SCARY STORIES

GHOULISH
GHOST STORIES

By Joan Axelrod-Contrada

Consultant:
Simon J. Bronner, PhD
Distinguished Professor of American Studies and Folklore
Fellow, American Folklore Society
The Pennsylvania State University, Harrisburg

CAPSTONE PRESS
a capstone imprint

Edge Books are published by Capstone Press,
151 Good Counsel Drive, P.O. Box 669, Mankato, Minnesota 56002.
www.capstonepub.com

Books published by Capstone Press are manufactured with paper
containing at least 10 percent post-consumer waste.

Library of Congress Cataloging-in-Publication Data
Axelrod-Contrada, Joan.
 Ghoulish ghost stories / by Joan Axelrod-Contrada.
   p. cm.—(Edge books. Scary stories)
 Includes bibliographical references and index.
 Summary: "Describes scary ghost stories, including The Bell Witch and
The Amityville Horror"—Provided by publisher.
 ISBN 978-1-4296-4574-4 (library binding)
 1. Ghosts—Juvenile literature. I. Title. II. Series.
BF1461.A96 2011
133.1—dc22   2010001364

Editorial Credits
Megan Peterson, editor; Ted Williams, designer; Kelly Garvin, media researcher;
    Laura Manthe, production specialist

Photo Credits
AP Images/Richard Drew, 21
Capstone Studio/Karon Dubke, scaremeter
copyright 1909 S.E. Guthrie, 14, 16
CORBIS/Bettmann, 18; Visions of America/Joseph Sohm, 10
Fortean Picture Library, 7, 29
Getty Images Inc./alek lindus, 23; Steve & Donna O'Meara, 26; Time & Life Pictures, 8
iStockphoto/shaunl, 4
Shutterstock/Allyson Ricketts, cover; Andrey Armyagov, 25; PHOTOCREO Michael
    Bednarek, 13

Design Elements
Shutterstock/averole (hand prints), Charles Taylor (rusty background), David M. Schrader
    (paper with tape), DCD (dribbles), Eugene Ivanov (border), George Nazmi Bebawi (fly),
    Gordan (borders), Hal_P (fingerprints), hfng (word bubble), Ian O'Ha (spider web), Kirsty
    Pargeter (brush strokes border), oxygen64 (frames), Ralf Juergen Kraft (computer bug),
    silver-john (paper), Subbotina Anna (fly), Thomas Bethge (tapes), xjbxjhxm123 (button)

TABLE OF CONTENTS

GRAB YOUR FLASHLIGHT

It's late at night, and you're sitting around the campfire. As the last flames flicker out, you shiver in the darkness. One of your friends begs you to hold a **séance**. Everyone joins hands and closes their eyes. You instruct your friends to breathe deeply in and out.

Suddenly you hear a knocking sound. A shadowy shape rises out of the smoke. It hovers over you and then disappears. Maybe there really *are* ghosts.

For thousands of years, some people have claimed to witness ghosts. Many believers say ghosts are the spirits of people who died tragically. These spirits may have unfinished business compelling them to haunt the living.

The popularity of ghost stories is nothing new. Almost 2,000 years ago, ancient Roman writer Pliny the Younger wrote about a chain-rattling ghost.

All of the ghost stories in this collection are tales that some people believe to be true. Others may wonder if they really happened. But no one can deny that these tales will send chills down your spine. Read on—if you dare.

 séance—a meeting at which people attempt to make contact with ghosts

THE HOUSE OF FLYING OBJECTS

SCARY

One February morning in 1967, something odd happened in the Cambridge, England, home of 11-year-old Matthew Manning. Matthew's father woke up to find his silver mug lying on the floor. He always kept the mug on a certain wooden shelf. Had one of his three children moved it in the middle of the night?

Matthew's father placed the mug back on the shelf. A few mornings later, he again found it on the floor. His children denied moving it.

Other objects mysteriously moved around the house. Silverware, plates, baskets, chairs, and ashtrays turned up in strange places. At first, no one saw them shift locations. Matthew's father wondered what could have caused these strange events. The police told him to contact the Cambridge Psychical Research Society.

Dr. George Owen, a **paranormal** expert, came to the Mannings' house to investigate. He blamed the moving objects on a **poltergeist**. This type of ghost is often found in households with children.

When Matthew went away to a private boarding school, nothing unusual happened at the house. But when he came home for spring break in 1971, the ghostly activity got worse. Much worse.

Poltergeists are believed to move or stack objects.

paranormal—something that can't be explained by science
poltergeist—a ghost that moves objects

One night Matthew woke up after hearing an odd scraping noise. He claimed his dresser edged toward him like a towering giant. His bed rose off the ground. Matthew leaped out of bed, shivering with fright. He later described the incident:

For thousands of years, people have reported poltergeist activity.

FEAR FACT

According to a 2007 U.S. survey, 34 percent of Americans believe in ghosts.

"I switched off the light and almost simultaneously my bed started to vibrate violently back and forth. I was now too timid to move, and I lay in anticipation of whatever might happen next. The vibrating ceased, and I felt the bottom end of my bed rising from the floor to what I estimated to be about one foot."

Soon other family members witnessed the flying objects. An eraser hovered in the air, and then it dropped to the floor. A shampoo bottle rocked back and forth on the edge of the bathtub. Hammers, coat hangers, and cans of paint flew up the staircase. Out of nowhere, the words "Matthew Beware" appeared on the walls.

The poltergeist followed Matthew back to his boarding school. At night, his bed moved around the boys' dormitory. Soon other students' beds began to move.

In his book *The Link*, Matthew described how he used the power of his own mind to tame the poltergeist. By channeling his energy into writing, he claimed to have driven away the force. Then again, maybe it just left to haunt someone else.

THE HAUNTED BRIDGE

VERY SCARY

NO TRUCKS OR BUSES ALLOWED
PER ORDER SELECTMEN

Emily's Bridge in
Stowe, Vermont

Imagine a female ghost with claws sharper than a tiger's. That's how people describe Emily's ghost in Stowe, Vermont.

Legend has it that Emily was a young woman shattered by a broken heart. One night in 1849, she went to the Gold Brook Bridge to meet the man of her dreams. But he never showed up. Emily's ghost is said to hover over the bridge where she was left waiting. After nightfall, people call it Emily's Bridge.

Through the years, some eerie events have been reported on the bridge. In 2001, a photographer wanted to capture Emily's ghost on film. But as soon as he stepped onto the bridge, his camera stopped working. The camera worked again once the photographer left the bridge.

FEAR FACT

In 1718, the famous pirate Blackbeard was killed off the coast of North Carolina. The bloody attack severed his head. According to legend, Blackbeard's headless body started to swim after it was tossed overboard. His ghost is said to hover over the spot where he died.

Around the same time, a man and some friends parked their car on Emily's Bridge. They saw a white light shaped like a woman slowly circle around the car. The man and his passengers scrambled to lock their doors. Suddenly something grabbed a door handle and shook the car. Everyone agreed it must be Emily's ghost.

In 2006, a married couple drove onto the bridge. The temperature in their car dropped, and they claimed something rocked and scratched their car. Was it Emily's ghost?

Even ghost hunters seem to be no match for Emily's ghost. One ghost hunter got out of her car in the inky darkness to approach the ghost. She wanted to help Emily's spirit move on. But the woman believed Emily became angry and attacked her. The woman later described the attack:

"A pain slowly settled into the back of my neck, while a pressure on the front made it difficult to breathe. The pain was excruciating, unbelievable."

Such incidents are said to occur only after sundown. So unless you are feeling very brave, stay away from Emily's Bridge in the dead of night.

FEAR FACT

Why are so many ghosts white? Some researchers say ghosts are pale because their blood has stopped flowing.

THE BELL WITCH

VERY SCARY

The Bell family claimed a ghost turned their home into a living nightmare.

Kate, known as the Bell Witch, was said to have the meanest laugh in all of Tennessee. "Hee-AW, Hee-AW, Hee-AW," she cackled.

Her real name was Kate Batts. Kate believed John Bell had cheated her out of a piece of land. Right before her death in the early 1800s, Kate promised to haunt the Bell family. She might have been true to her word.

One night in May 1818, the Bell children claimed they heard a scratching noise that sounded like rats gnawing on wood. They felt something yank their hair. Daughter Betsy heard a voice forbidding her to marry her boyfriend. Son Richard Williams Bell later recalled one of Kate's supposed attacks:

"The family had all retired early, and I had just fallen into a sweet doze when I felt my hair beginning to twist, and then a sudden jerk, which raised me. It felt like the top of my head had been taken off."

The Bell family asked the spirit to name itself but got no reply. When the family's preacher questioned the spirit, the ghost identified itself as "old Kate Batts' witch."

The Bell family believed Kate Batts' ghost poisoned John Bell with a strange liquid. When they tested the liquid on a cat, the cat died.

General Andrew Jackson, who later became a U.S. president, reportedly set out to see if the ghost really existed. The wagon carrying Jackson suddenly ground to a stop as it approached the Bells' house. The driver whipped the horses, but they wouldn't budge. Finally the general asked the ghost for permission to pass, and the horses continued.

Once Jackson entered the house, furniture and dishes began to fly around the rooms. A friend who claimed he could tame witches tried to kill Kate. He drew his pistol, but the gun would not fire. Before long, Jackson heard Kate's terrible cackle. He left in a fright.

The ghost tormented the Bell household from 1817 until 1821. John Bell fell victim to a number of strange illnesses. The ghost cursed at him every day, so he couldn't get any rest. He complained of a funny sensation in his mouth that made it difficult to eat.

John died on December 20, 1820. His breath smelled like the black liquid found in a strange bottle. No one had ever seen the bottle before. Had the Bell Witch poisoned him? No one will ever know for sure.

THE HOUSE OF HORRORS

A previous owner named the house at 112 Ocean Avenue "High Hopes."

On the night of November 13, 1974, 23-year-old Ronald DeFeo Jr. committed one of the most gruesome crimes in history. He shot and killed his parents and four siblings while they slept.

A year later, a realtor warned George and Kathy Lutz about the tragic past of the house on Ocean Avenue. But the spacious house in Amityville, New York, seemed like the perfect place to raise their three children. Besides, the Lutzes didn't believe in ghosts. Not at first, anyway.

The Lutzes claimed strange things happened soon after they moved into their seaside home. A priest came to bless the house. He stepped back in horror as a strange voice said, "Get out!" George complained of icy chills that made the house feel like a refrigerator. An awful green slime oozed from the ceiling.

The couple then discovered a closet in the basement. Behind it was a secret room painted red. It smelled like blood. Just as George was leaving the red room, he saw a shadowy figure against the wall.

The frightening events didn't stop once George and Kathy went to sleep. George kept waking up in the middle of the night, right around the time the murders had taken place. On the night of January 4, 1976, he lay awake in bed, unable to sleep. He crept downstairs and then heard heavy breathing coming from his bedroom. George raced back upstairs and found Kathy floating in the air. He quickly pulled her back down to the bed.

FEAR FACT

The hit TV show *Medium* is based on real-life **medium** Allison DuBois. Just like her TV character, DuBois has visions of the dead and helps the police find missing people.

The children also witnessed strange events. They found freshly cleaned toilet bowls filled with thick, black sludge. Their playroom became too cold to play in, even with the heat turned up. After 28 days, the family moved out of the house.

George and Kathy told their tale in the best-selling book *The Amityville Horror*. A movie based on the book made viewers shake with fright. Just hearing the words "Amityville Horror" is enough to make you scream.

medium—a person who claims to make contact with ghosts

Crime scene photo of the DeFeo murders

THE BOY WHO SEES GHOSTS

FREAKY SCARY

It all began with what seemed like just a bad dream. One windy fall night in the late 1990s, 9-year-old Michael Jones woke up screaming in the family's Connecticut home. His mother, Denice, ran into his bedroom. She found Michael trembling and in tears. He said a ghost had tried to touch his shoulder.

Was Michael acting strangely because his mother had recently gotten remarried? Was he mentally ill? Doctors declared Michael to be perfectly healthy.

At night, the spirits Michael called the "bad people" grew more and more terrifying. They threw toys across his room and yanked the covers off his bed. Family members took turns sleeping on a cot in his room to protect him. Still, Michael awoke with bloodcurdling screams.

Denice brought in a church group to bless the house, but their efforts failed. Objects rattled. The air turned icy cold. Red marks appeared on Michael's body. A foul smell like that of a dead animal wafted through the house. The words "Michael, we're coming to get you!" appeared on the wall above the stairwell. Next to it was a crudely drawn eye dripping red tears.

Shortly thereafter, the family moved into a new house. But it wasn't the house that was haunted—it was Michael! The bad spirits followed him to his new house. They wrote "Ha-ha. We've found you!" on his bedroom ceiling.

The ghost Michael named "the shadow man" was the worst of all the bad spirits. The dark outline of a man threatened to kill Michael. To save Michael's life, his family brought him to church for an **exorcism**. The priest prayed for the ghosts to leave Michael alone. But the shadow man refused to go away.

One Friday, Michael's older brother, Kenny, saw the shadow man on the basement stairs. The next night, Michael went to bed early. Denice remembered what happened next:

"Not even a half hour went by when he cried out. As I ran upstairs he screamed again, then the scream broke and there was silence as if he had stopped breathing. I rushed into his room, and Michael was gulping for air."

Michael told his mom that the shadow man had tried to strangle him. But the "good" spirits of his dead grandfather and friend made the bad spirit leave.

Michael says he continues to see ghosts. But he has learned to live with his unusual ability.

> **exorcism**—actions taken to rid a person or place of bad spirits

FEAR FACT

In an Irish myth, the ghost of a mean man named Stingy Jack roamed the night. He used a hollowed out turnip for a lantern. To scare away Stingy Jack, Irish people carved scary faces into turnips and potatoes and set them outside. They called them Jack of the Lanterns or jack- o'-lanterns.

THINGS THAT
GO BUMP IN
THE NIGHT

Truth can be stranger than fiction—and a lot scarier too! But are ghosts real? It's hard to say. Paranormal researchers use high-tech gadgets to check for evidence of ghostly activity. Thermal imaging cameras locate the hot and cold spots thought to be caused by paranormal activity. Motion sensors are said to detect the movements of ghosts.

Skeptics scoff at scientific proof of ghosts. They think people imagine ghosts or make up wild stories for fame and fortune. In the case of *The Amityville Horror*, the Lutz's tale was turned into a best-selling book and movie. After the book's release, Ronald DeFeo Jr.'s lawyer came forward and claimed he helped the Lutzes make up the story. Other people also claimed the story was a **hoax**.

 hoax—a trick to make people believe something that is not true

Sometimes what seems like a ghost turns out to be something else. For instance, someone can make an eerie-looking photograph by putting a fingerprint on the **negative**. Small insects or specks of dust can appear as white shapes on flash photos. And low-hanging tree branches are sometimes to blame for those mysterious noises that go bump in the night.

PERFECT YOUR SCARY STORYTELLING

To perfect your own scary storytelling, think of what gives you the creeps. Choose a scary setting, and put your main character in danger. Maybe she's trapped in a dark movie theater, or he's stuck in a haunted house. Play up the spooky sights, sounds, and smells of the night. Create suspense by unfolding details about who the ghost is.

Do you need more time to come up with the next part of the story? Ask your listeners, "And do you know what happened next?" Now turn off the lights, pull down the shades, and get ready to make your friends' scalps tingle with fright.

In 1995, a photographer took this photo of a burning building in Shropshire, England. He claimed the girl in the doorway is a ghost.

FEAR FACT

Millions of people tune into reality TV shows like *Ghost Hunters*. As a result, ghost-hunting groups and spooky tours are more popular than ever before.

negative—a photographic film used to make photos

GLOSSARY

exorcism (EK-sur-siz-uhm)—actions taken to rid a person or place of bad spirits

hoax (HOHKS)—a trick to make people believe something that is not true

medium (MEE-dee-um)—a person who claims to make contact with ghosts

negative (NEG-uh-tiv)—a photographic film used to make photos; a negative shows light areas as dark and dark areas as light

paranormal (pa-ruh-NOR-muhl)—something that can't be explained by science

poltergeist (POLE-tuhr-gyst)—a ghost that is believed to make loud noises and to move objects

séance (SAY-ohnss)—a meeting at which people attempt to make contact with ghosts

skeptic (SKEP-tik)—a person who doubts things that other people believe in

spirit (SPIHR-it)—the invisible part of a person that contains thoughts and feelings; some people believe the spirit leaves the body after death

Gee, Joshua. *Encyclopedia Horrifica: The Terrifying Truth! about Vampires, Ghosts, Monsters, and More.* New York: Scholastic Inc., 2007.

Olson, Arielle North, and Howard Schwartz. *More Bones: Scary Stories from around the World.* New York: Viking, 2008.

Shores, Lori. *Ghosts: Truth and Rumors.* Truth and Rumors. Mankato, Minn.: Capstone Press, 2010.

Teitelbaum, Michael. *Ghosts and Real-Life Ghost Hunters.* 24/7 Science Behind the Scenes. New York: Franklin Watts, 2008.

INTERNET SITES

FactHound offers a safe, fun way to find Internet sites related to this book. All of the sites on FactHound have been researched by our staff.

Here's all you do:

Visit *www.facthound.com*

Type in this code: 9781429645744

INDEX